Scotland's Storie[s]

This book is a gift to you f[rom] ~~a national charity changing~~ lives through reading and writing, to celebrate Book Week Scotland (17–23 November 2025).

bookweekscotland.com

Friendship is a collection of true stories written by the people of Scotland. This book is one of 70,000 **free** copies – thank you for picking it up! If you enjoy it, help us share it with as many people as possible. Dip into it and share a few favourites with friends, display it, gift a copy to a partner, colleague or parent, or even leave it somewhere for a stranger to discover.
(We recommend a reading age of 15+.)

These stories are both funny and moving, paying tribute to the breadth of storytelling across multiple generations all over Scotland. If you enjoy this book, please consider making a donation so that everyone in Scotland has the opportunity to improve their life chances through books and the fundamental skills of reading and writing.

Visit **scottishbooktrust.com/donate** to find out more.

Happy reading!
#BookWeekScotland

A huge thank you to the following individuals who supported Scottish Book Trust as members of The Book Club

Martin Adam and William Zachs

Christian Albuisson

Gordon Dalyell and Pamela Leslie

Marian and Mark Deere

Scott Lothian

and those who wish to remain anonymous

Friendship

Scottish
Book Trust

scottishbooktrust.com

First published in 2025 by Scottish Book Trust,
Sandeman House, Trunk's Close, 55 High Street,
Edinburgh EH1 1SR

scottishbooktrust.com

The authors' right to be identified as an author of this book under
the Copyright, Patents and Designs Act 1988 has been asserted

A CIP catalogue record for this book is available
from the British Library

Typeset by Craig Laurenson

Printed and bound by CPI Group (UK) Ltd, Croydon CR0 4YY

Scottish Book Trust makes every effort to ensure that the paper
used in this book has been legally sourced from well-managed
and sustainable forests

Cover design by Craig Laurenson

This is a free book, designed to be read alone or in groups, enjoyed,
shared and passed on to friends. This book is gifted to you by
Scottish Book Trust for Book Week Scotland 2025

Digital editions of this book are available from
scottishbooktrust.com

Contents

Formative friendships

Community friendships

Friends we found in difficult moments

50 Word Non-Fiction

Friends for life

Unexpected friendships

*Stories by published authors.

Please be aware that this book is unsuitable for readers aged 14 or younger as it contains strong language and mature content.

Formative friendships

Past Tense
Judith Younger

The farmers around us burned the gorse that autumn,
perfect for girls who had decided to be witches. We
scarred our faces black with broken charcoaled stumps.

We found a jag-toothed oil drum for our cauldron. We
wrote careful spells with much underlining in old maths
jotters.

You found a dead crow with one wing, and we threw
it in with leaves and rosehip seedpods, stirring and
chanting like we thought witches should.

You said to take our boots off, so we danced barefoot
and screamed our spells at startled rabbits. Spells to
capture dark-eyed Ewan in the year above; to make my
boobs grow bigger; to give that cow Michelle pustuled
acne everywhere.

Afterwards, we smoked stolen cinnamon sticks,
watching the dry ends crackle as we coughed. We spat
on our palms and swore friendship forever.

When our mums called us for tea, we squeezed further
behind the fractured branches, scrabbling in stones and
dust, held hands and waited for the moon.

*

The gorse on Calton Hill is dayglow yellow and creeps
coconut on our arms as we drag through. Sometimes we
can only manage half an hour in our lunch break.

One day last summer, a huge fire had stripped the
bushes, curling thick golden flames like lava over the
rock, painting new shadows on the smooth monument
pillars. It had taken hours to make it safe. But we were

too old to play in the sooty remains, too tired to chant and dance.

We sit on a bench and look out to sea, and you say you wonder where the spells are now. Where are the ones to heal the pain and stop the torment, and find the lost?

I hold your hand and know you don't want any words.

*

But today you are smiling and say let's go to the Meadows, and we walk through grass, kicking dandelion heads, see them float like leftover breath. We have prosecco in paper cups. You take off your shoes to stretch out your toes and tell me he is home. Your boy has come back, he is free of his father, and there is new life after all.

We sit on a rug and hug quietly, with joyful tears. We laugh to remember the spells, and you point at my now sagging chest.

And we don't want to leave. We hold hands and wait for the moon.

Author note: *Talking with a friend going through a difficult time and remembering fondly how we used to play witches as children, and wondering if our spells would still work.*

Càirdeas
Peter Mackay

Dè a th'ann? Deich thar fhichead bliadhna o
chaidh sinn a' campadh ann an Tolastadh 's air
a' Bhràighe: meanbh-chuileagan, fuachd an t-
samhraidh, sleeping bags, sliasaid ri sliasaid,
craiceann ri craiceann, fàileadh cùbhraidh
fiodh air an teine agus, seadh, bruadaran na h-
òige agus cinnt gun robh a h-uile càil fhathast
romhainn. Bruadaran: aig teampall Asclepius,
Dia an leigheis, ann an Trikala, bhiodh iad a'
dèanamh an adhraidh do Mnemosyne, màthair
nan ceòlraidhean, leis an dòchas gum biodh i
gad chuideachadh aisling sam bith a bh'agad
agus ann an sin a chuimhneachadh. 'S e
slànachadh a bhiodh ann an sin, 's dòcha, ach
cha chreid mi g' eil an ìomhaigh buileach
ìomchaidh an-dràsta 's mi a' feuchainn ri guth
mo bhàrdachd a thoirt nas fhàisge ri mo ghuth
àbhaisteach, ge bith dè a tha sin a' ciallachadh,
dè seòrsa pasgan cèidse no cliabh a th'ann. Ach
tha e a' faireachdainn cudromach dhomh nach
b' iad caractaran mo chuimhn' a-mhàin a bh'
anns an triùir againn a' bleadraigeadh fon
ghealaich air an tràigh mar chràbhaichean as
dèidh na seirbhis, agus gur ann an dà-rìribh a
tha sinn an seo a-nochd, ann an taigh-bidh' a'
coimhead ciaradh an fheasgair a' muthadh cala
Steòrnabhaigh, fhathast na h-aon cleasan agus
obagan a bh' againne riamh ri fhaicinn: do
theanga, agus thu a' tarraing asainn, a' tighinn
nas fhàide a-mach nad bheul na shaoillin 's a

4

bhiodh comasach, agus thusa, do chorragan
glaiste mar mhullach theampaill, gàire bhragail
air d'aodann agus ceistean ro choileanta, ro
phearsanta an-còmhnaidh air do liopan. Tha e
doirbh a ràdh dè a tha thu ag ionndrainn gus
am bi e air do beulaibh, a' suidhe timcheall
bòrd còmhla riut, aig ithe Yum Gai Yang, gach
facal mar shnàithlean tìm a' ruith tro luchairt-
cuimhne. Duilich? Agus mis', ciamar a tha mis'
faighinn air adhart? An d'fhuair mi toileachas
riamh? Dè am bruadar a bha agam air a'
Bhràighe? An e an triùir againn a bh'ann? Hut.
Deich thar fhichead bliadhna, tha thu 'g ràdh?

Friendship

What is it? Thirty years since we camped in
Tolsta and on the Bràighe: midges and the
summer cold, sleeping bags, thighs against
thighs, skin against skin, the smell of fenceposts
– stolen strainers – on the fire and, yes, those
were the dreams of youth and everything still in
front of us. Dreams. At the temple in Trikala to
Asclepius, the god of medicine, they also paid
worship to Mnemosyne, mother of the muses,
in the belief she could help you remember any
vision you had while sleeping there. That could
be a healing of sorts, but does not seem the
right register here, as I try to bring the voice of
my poetry closer to my speaking voice,
whatever that bundle, that creel might be,
because it feels important that those three
people blethering on the beach in the moonlight

like worshippers after a service are not just
inventions of my memory, and that we are really
all here tonight, in a restaurant watching the
dusk like incense smothering Stornoway
Harbour, still with the same tics and habits we
ever had: your tongue when you're taking the
piss coming further out of your mouth than is
surely possible; your fingers pressed together
like a temple roof, an impish smile on your face
as you ask too perfect, too personal questions.
It is hard to say what you have missed until it is
there, sitting round a table with you, eating Yum
Gai Yang, each word a thread of time leading
through a memory palace. Sorry? And me, how
am I getting on? Did I ever find happiness? What
was that dream on the Bràighe? Was it actually
us three? Hut. Thirty years ago, you say?

Juice Tigers
Robbie Handy

What does a fifteen-year-auld boy hae in common wi a fifty-year-auld man?

Well, if they're the same person, turns oot it could be a fair bit.

On any given day, I can look doon (and peer oot ower ma belly) tae see a reassuring pair o Nike Air Max 1s or Adidas Kicks on ma feet.

I can batter away at a heavy bag at the gym – daeing the same vague impression o a boxer I've done for decades.

And I can catch a snatch o 'I Am the Resurrection' by The Stone Roses on the radio – long-lost teenage romances and fights taking flight wi the chorus.

But as I approach my half-century, my life force is sustained by somethin stronger than clathes, movement and memories. And somethin less nebulous than nostalgia. It's powered by the flesh and blood brothers peekin ower the precipice with me.

They aw ken who they are, so I'll no list them oot. In 1992 we formed a gang. Well, it was supposed tae be an anti-gang, really. Cos maist o the gangs in Dunfermline back then were based on supportin the same fitbaw team. Or liking the same clathes. Or coming fae the same area or village. Or lovin the same music. We were borne by bits o aw they things, but bound by something bigger: first and foremost, we were real mates.

The type o mates who ayways had each other's backs. The type o mates who would sacrifice oor safety for each other. The type o mates ye stuck by nae matter what – because even if there were spells ye didnae 100% like each other, ye ayways loved one another.

That's what happens when pals become brothers. And friends become faimly. In the decades since, we've stuck thegether through breakups, breakdoons and deaths. Raised glasses for milestones, marriages and births. And been there for aw the wee bits in between that weave lives intae each other.

So here's tae The Juice Tigers.

Named efter a long-defunct American juice blender that had a belter o an advert on Sell-a-Vision.

We've gone fae tearaway paper boys tae stick o rock men.

Hedge hoppers tae mortgage proppers.

Mad chancers tae dad dancers.

Received wisdom is that if ye're the same at fifty as ye were at fifteen, ye've wasted yer life.

But I'm no sure aboot that.

Because the fifty-year-aulds I see who've changed the maist are often the ones who feel the maist deid.

But the ones who've smuggled their fifteen-year-auld selves through the mangle o adulthood still have that vital spark aboot them.

That's what's different wi us boys.

The wild-eyed love that made us cut oor thumbs and swear loyalty tae each other is still in oor blood three decades later.

Aye, the fifteen-quid Juice Tigers tattoo I got fae Jaggy Jim has faded. But still, its colours dinnae run.

Maikin Life Curly
William Letford

Thi earliest pals a remembur hivin wur ma grandparents.
Oan thi first Friday eh ivery month, ma sister an me wid be
packed off tae stiy it thur hoose. This wiz a point a contention
wae ma parents. Ma faither wid say, They full thur heeds
wae mad coo's shite, aw that nonsense might change thum
furiver. Ma mam wid simply reply, Nothin wrong wae
maikin life curly. Ma nana an papa moved aboot thur hoose
like they hid landed oan earth fae some far-off dusty part eh
thi universe. Thur decrepitude wiz otherworldly. Ma eyes wur
young back then, that's a perspective a can niver change.
In ma memory, thur raisin-skinned, gummy-eyed, an iz
distant an beautiful iz constellations in a clear, midnight sky.
Ma papa loved talcum pooder. Thur wiz clouds eh it left
in thi bathroom efter eed showered. Ma sister, whose bladdur
iwiys seemed tae be heavy wae piss, wid rush intae thi
bathroom efter um an come oot clappin white an coaffin.
Ma nana constantly hud a cigarette danglin fae r first
two fingers. A wid sit croass-legged oan thi livin room flair
an watch thi glowing tip zig n zag iz she used r hands
tae illustrate one eh r long meanderin stories. Despite thi
talcum pooder in thi bathroom an thi cigarette ash
in thi soup, a remember they days like thur wiz conjury
in thi world they created fur us. We wur niver sent tae bed.
We'd faw asleep where we sat an wake up wae a pulla
beneath oor heeds an a blanket tucked aroond us. Freedom.
They allowed us tae stiy up late because they loved thi night.
A think they loved thi night because life could shrink tae
Friday evenin television, a coal fire, an a torrent a stories
thit, sometimes, hud a wisp eh thi truth. Once, when thi coal
in thi fire burned brighter than thi lamps, they taught ma
sister an me how tae dance. Move yur boady any wiy yi wish,
they sade, jist smile while yi dae it. Aw thi walllflowers will

be in awe eh yur confidence, an truly jealous eh how much yur enjoyin yursel. In this respect, ma faither wiz correct. Ma sister an me r thi worst an best dancers it thi pairty.

Càirdeas na Cloinne
Victoria Niclomhair

7, 6, 5, 4, 3, 2, 1.
Is sinn uile ar seasamh seasgair
deiseil is deònach 'son a' chamara.
Faitichean-gàire a' bobadaich
mar na tuinn luainiche.

Teaghlaichean cruinn còmhla
a' gagadaich mar gheòidh.
Sheas sinn, deic de chairtean, sreath
a' taisbeanadh ar n-aoisean mar bhràistean.
Ach,

chì mi bus làn sonas a' falbh dhan tràigh.
M' antaidh is Mam a' draibheadh.
A' bhòrd làn biadh is bodhaigean.

Gheibh mi fàileadh cè-ghrèine mhilis
le beagan gràinean saillte.
Feur is flùraichean air cuairtean samhraidh.

Cluinnidh mi an t-òran co-là-breith
ga sheinn gu mì-mhodhail.
Sgreuchail is ùpraid bhon ghàrradh.

Tha e crochte air balla cidsin mo mhàthair.
An glainne rèidh fo mo mheòir
seachd co-oghaichean
agus ar n-òige
air a ghlacadh gu siorraidh.

Childhood Friendship

7, 6, 5, 4, 3, 2, 1.
All standing together snugly,
ready and willing for the camera.
Smiles bobbing up and down,
like restless waves.

Families all together
gaggling like geese.
We stood, a deck of cards, all in line,
our ages displayed like badges.
But,

I can see a bus full of joy heading for the beach.
My auntie and mum driving,
the table groaning with food and bodies.

The smell of sweet sunscreen
mingled with salty sand.
Grass and flowers on summer trips.

I hear the birthday song
being sung cheekily.
Screams and uproar coming from the garden.

It hangs on my mum's kitchen wall.
The glass smooth to my touch.
Seven cousins and our youth
captured forever.

Author note: *This is inspired by the close friendship my siblings and I had with our cousins growing up. We entered the local fancy dress competition for the Summer*

Gala as a deck of cards, displaying our consecutive ages. The faded photo hangs still on my parents' kitchen wall, capturing a glimpse of our friendships and the taste of summers gone by.

Community friendships

Tuna Sandwiches
Mhairi Kelly

They never exchanged soft words.
As they never learned how to express their feelings.

Not when they were only boys in overalls, knees deep in
grease, grafting all those back-punishing hours,
while serving their time.
Pushing each other to make it through.
Not when they bought houses on opposite ends of the
same scheme.
Regular visits for tea were all that were needed.
Not when they held each other's newborns like
something sacred and breakable.
A handshake would do.
Not during times of grief.
When each set of parents died, one by one,
quiet was the way they clapped the other's back.

Yet they met every Saturday.
Always.
After the football,
after the shouting across the field or at the telly –
which meant nothing,
and everything.
The dog knew the route by heart.
The bench recognised their weight.

Every second Saturday, I'd join them and admire their
unwavering bond.
The childish banter and the ease of conversation.
Wishing I'd form a connection to last as long.

Every week, it was the same thing.
He brought tuna sandwiches –
since he was young, it was his favourite.
Now it was packed by a wife who read the labels,
watched the salt, and worried about his heart.
The other brought meat, eggs, cheese – a different kind
every week, as if variety was rebellion.
They'd swap halves.
A quiet ritual.
No words for affection,
this was their shared thing.

Because in their actions, they proved their loyalty.
In showing up, they provided strength.
In silence, they heard all the other needed to say.
In each other's company, they found comfort.

And that was love.

Time passed the way it does – slow, then sudden.
Illness crept in.
Gentle at first, before it took hold.
His friend walked slower than usual, taking more breaks
on their journey.
All too soon, the tradition faded.
And one Saturday, his friend was gone.
Their lives once parallel now marked by the distance
grief had carved.

I couldn't give him back what was taken.
But I could make sure he didn't walk their path alone.

So it's the same time every Saturday.
The same walk, same bench.

I bring the tuna.
He still brings the surprise.

We sit, swap halves,
and in that silent offering,
I feel the resonance of a lifetime – of history,
of the kind of love men like them were never taught to name,
but carried anyway,
in sandwiches,
with silence,
and showing up.
In their routine and now in memory.

We say nothing of what was lost, only share what remains.

Author note: *My dad and I share a dog walk each weekend. We regularly meet older men who enjoy chatting, often seeking a bit of company. This piece is inspired by the stories they tell, the memories they share, and the time we spend with them. I wrote this poem to give myself some closure, as I often worry about the old and lonely. I'd like to think we make a difference to their week, as they are a fond part of ours.*

The Driver on the 6.18 Bus
Elizabeth Clingan

I was the only passenger to get on at Lanark.

He and I chatted about the weather, as strangers often do. He wasn't as enthusiastic about the recent good weather as I was. Looking into the sun made driving harder and he had got sunburnt on his right arm the day before.

He did this run every day, whatever the weather.

A man wearing an anorak and looking a bit flustered got on at the bottom of the High Street.
　'Morning pal, how are you this morning? You're looking a bit stressed.'
　'I'm all right mate – just thought I was going to miss you.'

The bus swung out of Lanark, a loud toot of the horn, an extravagant wave, 'Hiya, pal.'
　Pal was unlikely to have heard anything but waved back in recognition and continued on his dog walk.

Pink-jacket lady got on in Braidwood. At the bus stop she'd been talking to a young lad all in black with his hoodie up who looked as if he needed people to talk to him. He was now bent over his phone.
　'Morning, pal. How was your day off yesterday?'
　'It was great, I was in the garden all day.'
　'Lucky for some!'

Anorak man got off in Carluke and hurried off somewhere – to work probably. I wondered which place in Carluke started work at 7am.

'Cheers,' he said brightly as the bus doors opened. Managing to catch the bus had clearly lightened his mood.

'See you Monday, pal.'

A young woman was waiting at the next stop. She asked something about the fare.

'What time are you coming back at? Tell you what, get this ticket and that'll save you a wee bit.'

'Thanks so much,' she said and sat down, smiling.

Ten minutes later, she pressed the stop button and got off beside Wishaw General, clutching her NHS identity badge.

'Cheerio, pal. You have a good day now.'

Then it was striped-trouser lady.

'Good to see you, pal. How you doing? Glad it's Friday?'

'Certainly am, it's been a long week. Do you have tomorrow off?'

'I've one run to do in the morning and then that's me. Afternoon in front of the telly with the remote all to myself.'

A few stops later, donkey jacket and hi-vis lads got on.

'Where are they sending you lads today, then?'

'Over to Cumbernauld. We have to take some scaffolding down.'

'That'll no' be fun in this heat.'

'I think your team is going to get thrashed tomorrow.'

'That'll no' be happening, pal.'

We approached Strathclyde University, where pink-jacket lady got off.

'You have a good weekend, pal. See you Monday.'

'You too. See you.'

The bus pulled into Buchanan Street.

The rest of us got off and headed on to wherever we were headed.

'Bye, pal.'

'See ya, pal.'

'Take care, pal.'

Soon he would turn his bus round to head back to Lanark and be a pal all over again.

Author note: *This was inspired by a bus journey I took from Lanark to Glasgow. I was very taken by the way the driver had chat for everyone and that, alongside the Scottish use of 'pal' (not used like this where I come from), made me think that this is also friendship. The importance of really close friends is well-documented, but I think we also need to recognise the importance of these friendly exchanges. They demonstrate friendship too.*

Wednesdays at 10am
Laura M Pearson

I opened the door and walked in backwards, pulling the pram behind me. I was still learning to manoeuvre it through small spaces, a skill that would become second nature in a few months, but I didn't realise that yet. I still felt overly cautious about the delicate wee bundle inside.

I approached the reception, slightly flustered, and asked for directions to the Baby Group. It had been a busy morning of dirty nappies, milky cuddles and a long, drawn-out process of getting us both washed and dressed – all building up to this point. I was pleased I had made it here. I had done it, I was out of the house with my baby.

'That's where I'm heading,' I heard a voice call. 'You can walk down with me.'

The voice belonged to a lady with long blonde tousled hair and a huge grin. She had a baby strapped to her chest in a multi-coloured fabric wrap and a small toddler who was running ahead of her down a long corridor.

'Thanks,' I called, pushing the pram over to her, feeling clumsy and a bit like someone playing a character in comparison to her calm, Mother Earth aura.

'You're early,' she said as we walked. 'You can help me set up if that's OK? I'm Charli.'

She opened the doors to a large sports hall, with soft foam mats covering two-thirds of the floor. The toddler started to run in circles around the hall.

As I parked up the pram, I glanced in to see my baby still sleeping. It was such a relief when he slept, I could relax briefly, and I felt like I was finally doing something right. I used the freedom to help Charli pull toys out of the cupboard, listening to her chat and following instructions on placing the toys.

The room started to fill up with other parents and kids. The volume increased, and I hovered around the pram nervously, waiting for the unfamiliar noises to jolt my baby awake, anticipating the tears I had grown to expect. But he stayed soundly asleep.

'Here, take this,' a biscuit and a mug were pushed towards me. 'No milk, you said, right? I made it strong. Enjoy it while you can. He's adorable. How old?'

'Thirteen weeks and two days,' I replied.

'Aw, this wee one's about the same,' she gestured at the baby snuggled in the carrier.

'Does she sleep well?' I asked wearily, wincing at the memory of pacing the floors in the darkness, trying to soothe his screams. 'I feel like I'm doing it all wrong.' I felt my throat tighten and tears prick at my eyes.

'She's my second, so it's a bit less worrying. But they're all their own wee people. Oh, I think that's him awake. Come over here when you're ready.'

She introduced me to a group of women, all holding babies of various sizes. I settled into the group and listened to the conversation already in full flow as my baby's mouth found my breast. These women were voicing the concerns and anxieties I was experiencing as a first-time mum.

'Why are my nipples so sore?'

'How do I know what the crying means?'

'I am so tired, I put the kettle in the fridge and the milk carton on the worktop.'

I felt a weight lift from my shoulders. I wasn't doing it wrong, none of us were. We were learning and trying, and figuring it out as we went along. We were realising that the expectations we'd had of what motherhood would be like were different from reality. We'd been led to believe babies slept when they were tired, breastfeeding was a doddle, and being a mum was full of joy and love when, actually, a lot of it consisted of sleep deprivation and self-doubt. Two hours of honesty with this group of ladies had helped me feel understood, and it reassured me, knowing there were other people whom I could talk to.

I was smiling as I pushed my pram towards the door, the wee one tucked contentedly into his blankets.

'Will you be back next week?' Charli had asked, pushing a piece of folded paper into my hand.

'Yes, definitely,' I replied, unfolding the paper and seeing her phone number and name scrawled in blue biro.

'Good,' she said. 'It's a lovely group. I think you'll enjoy it.'

As the weeks passed, I felt a growing comfort and familiarity as I walked through the door. We greeted each other with the warm smiles and kindness of old friends. We cooed over babies' achievements and recognised the signs of a sleepless night. We knew how valuable the hand of friendship was, as new parents, and we tried our best to give our kindness generously, when we could. We were all in this together.

Attending this group allowed me to enjoy friendship every week without planning. Trying to explain to old friends that I was too tired for a night out, arranging meet-ups around nap times, or being late because of an unexpected nappy explosion, often brought me feelings of stress, guilt and letting people down. Sometimes it was easier not to try.

I learned that these weekly friendships gave me something to look forward to. A warm greeting, remembering details from something I'd said last week and asking about them, holding space for me when I'd had a bad week. Allowing me the chance to give the same in return. Those were the friends who supported me through my first year as a mum. They were the ones who kept me smiling, kept me hoping, and kept me going. They were indeed a lovely group. In fact, I'd say they were my lifeline.

Author note: *I felt overwhelmed and out of my depth as a new mum, struggling with breastfeeding and sleepless nights. Going to a local baby group helped me make connections with other people in the same position, and those friendships were a lifeline for me.*

An Drochaid
Graham Cooper

Bha an oidhche ann. Ach ann an uàrd-ospadail 5B
cha robh Tòmas MacIlleDhuibh na chadal, bha e ag
èisteachd ris a' ghaoith a' sèideadh.

Bha am fuaim a' toirt gu chuimhne oidhche gharbh
bho làithean òige, oidhche na stoirm uabhasaich ud –
ach cha robh eagal air a bhith air a chionn 's gun robh e
còmhla ri athair.

Dh'èirich Tòmas gus an robh e na shuidhe air
oir na leapa. Bha e air togail a thoirt dha a bhith a'
cuimhneachadh air athair – bha e air beagan fois a thoirt
da inntinn agus bha fadachd air a-nis gus an innseadh e
an naidheachd aige do chuideigin.

Bha an triùir eile anns an uàrd bheag nan cadal.

Chuir e air na slapagan aige agus thòisich e air
coiseachd. Bha an seann duine aig prìomh-dhoras an
uàird mus fhaca a' Bhanaltram Eilidh Nic a' Ghobhainn
e.

'Càit' a bheil sibh a' dol, a Thòmais?' dh'fhaighnich i.

Chlisg e. 'A Thòmais'! Cha bhiodh banaltram òg mar
Eilidh Nic a' Ghobhainn a' cleachdadh ainm baistidh
mar sin nuair a bha e na àrd-lighiche anns an ospadal.

'Tha mi a' dol a bhruidhinn rim athair,' fhreagair e.
'Tha deagh naidheachd agam.'

Ghnog Eilidh a ceann. 'Ceart gu leòr, a Thòmais,
ach tha e còig uairean sa mhadainn. Carson nach
till sibh dhan leabaidh 'son treis. Bidh an troilidh a'
tighinn timcheall aig sia uairean le cupa teatha dhuibh.
Dh'fhaodadh sibh an naidheachd agaibh innse dhan a
h-uile duine an uair sin.'

Lean a' bhanaltram Tòmas fhad 's a bha e a' tilleadh

dhan t-seòmar aige. Sgioblaich i an leabaidh. 'Mus
tèid sibh a chadal, a Thòmais, bu toigh leam tomhas a
dhèanamh air an ogsaidean san fhuil agaibh. Am biodh
sin ceart gu leòr?'

Chuir i an t-inneal-tomhais air tè de a chorragan.

'Tha an t-ogsaidean agaibh gu math ìosal, a Thòmais,'
thuirt Eilidh. 'Bidh fios agaibh dè tha sin a' ciallachadh
on a bha sibh fhèin nur lighiche. Dh'fhaodadh an cion-
ogsaidein a bhith gur cur troimh-a-chèile. Bu toigh leam
ogsaidean a thoirt dhuibh tro na 'nasal cannulas' seo.
Am biodh sin ceart gu leòr?'

Dhùin Tòmas a shùilean. Cha b' urrainn dha càil a
chluinntinn a-nis ach siosarnaich an ogsaidein anns na
pìoban.

Cha robh e a' còrdadh ris idir a bhith na euslainteach
anns an ospadal seo far an robh e air a bhith na
chomhairliche-leighis fad mòran bhliadhnaichean.
Choisinn e cliù dha fhèin mar lighiche air leth math ach,
on a leig e dheth a dhreuchd, b' ann ainneamh a thàinig
na co-obraichean aige faisg air. Bha e air fàs aonaranach.

An uair sin, o chionn sia mìosan, thòisich e air
casadaich. Nochd an fhuil. Nuair a thug e sùil air a'
ghath-x de na sgamhanan aige fhèin, cha robh iongnadh
air. Bha fios aige cheana dè an t-ainm a bha air an
tinneas aige. Cha robh saoghal fada roimhe.

Bha siosarnaich an ogsaidein ga chur na chadal…

Bha na dotairean agus na h-oileanaich mheidigeach
a' dèanamh cuairt-uàird, ach cha b' urrainn dhomh
càil fhaicinn ach balla de dhromannan air an robh
còtaichean geala. Carson a bha iad gam chur ann an
suarachas, agus mise nam àrd-lighiche os cionn na
roinne seo?

Mì-mhodh! Thionndaidh mi air mo shàil, agus rinn mi
air prìomh-dhoras an uàird.

Air taobh eile an dorais, ghabh mi frith-rathad a bha a' dol sìos tro choille-ghiuthais.

Fhad 's a bha mi a' cromadh a' bhruthaich, thug mi an aire gun robh fuaim mar thàirneanach, no toirm nan uisgeachan, a' fàs na b' àirde agus na b' àirde.

Cha b' fhada gus an do ràinig mi oir na coille agus an d' fhuair mi mi fhìn nam sheasamh air bearradh, àrd os cionn aibhne mhòir bheucaich.

B' ann an uair sin a chunnaic mi an drochaid.

B' i drochaid-chrochaidh thairis air an abhainn a bha ann. Cha robh rùm air a' cheum ach do choisiche leis fhèin agus, gus an gnothach a dhèanamh na b' eagalaiche buileach, bha grunn math de dhèilean a' cheuma a dhìth. Bha i mar dhrochaid a chitheadh sibh ann am film fantasach.

A dh'aindeoin sin, bha rud air choreigin gam tharraing, gam thàladh chun na drochaid. Bha fios agam gum feumainn a dhol thairis oirre.

Bha eagal orm nuair a chuir mi mo chas dheas air a' chiad dèile ged a bha i seasmhach gu leòr. Ach thug mi sùil air thoiseach orm fhìn agus b' i mearachd mhòr a bha sin. Chunnaic mi fear a' tuiteam sìos bho bhogha na drochaid, a ghàirdeanan a' bualadh an adhair mar sgiathan gun fheum. Chaidh e às an t-sealladh anns an abhainn dhomhainn. Ma rinn e sgreuch, cha chuala mi e.

An dèidh sin, chùm mi mo shùilean air a' cheum agus chaidh mi air adhart, mo chridhe a' plosgartaich.

Aig àird a' bhogha, cha mhòr nach do thuit mi bhàrr na drochaid, bha a leithid de thuaineal orm. Bha mo chasan air chrith. Ghabh mi grèim cho teann den ròpa-làimhe 's gun robh mi an dùil gun spreadhadh m' fhèithean.

Ach ràinig mi an taobh thall agus chuir mi mo chasan

air carraig.

Fhad 's a bha mi a' gabhail m' analach, thug mi an aire gun robh taigh mòr air fàire. Thog mi orm air an fhrith-rathad dha ionnsaigh.

Bha doras-aghaidh an taighe fosgailte agus choisich mi sìos trannsa agus a-steach do sheòmar farsaing far an robh cuideachd mhòr ri còmhradh. A rèir coltais, bha bangaid gu bhith ann.

Thàinig e a-steach orm gun robh mi a' dèanamh aithne gun chuimhne air na daoine a bha an làthair. Ach chuir e iongnadh orm nuair a chunnaic mi m' athair fhèin nam measg. Smèid e rium.

Bha mi a' coiseachd a dh'ionnsaigh m' athar le gàirdeachas nuair a chuala mi fuaim mar chupa a' dèanamh gliong air sàsar – chuir mi cùl ris.

Ann an uàrd 5B, bha tè air tighinn a thairgsinn cupa teatha do na h-euslaintich.

'Am bu toigh leibh cupa teatha, a Thòmais?' dh'fhaighnich i.

'A Thòmais?'

'A Thòmais…'

The Bridge

It was night. But in hospital ward 5B, Thomas Brown wasn't sleeping, he was listening to the wind blowing.

The sound reminded him of a wild night from his childhood, the night of that terrible storm – but he hadn't been afraid because he was with his father.

Thomas sat up on the edge of the bed. It had given him a lift to remember his father – it had given him some peace of mind – and now he was impatient to tell his news to someone.

The three others in the small ward were sleeping.

He put his slippers on and began to walk. The elderly man was at the main door of the ward before Nurse Helen Smith saw him.

'Where are you going, Tom?' she asked.

He jumped. 'Tom' indeed! Young nurses like Helen Smith would never have used his Christian name when he was a senior physician at the hospital.

'I'm going to speak to my father,' he replied. 'I have some good news.'

Helen nodded. 'OK, Tom, but it's five o'clock in the morning. Why don't you go back to bed for a little while? The trolley will be coming round at six with a cup of tea for you. You could tell your good news to everybody then.'

The nurse followed Thomas as he returned to his room. She tidied up his bed. 'Before you go to sleep, Tom, I'd like to measure your blood oxygen sats. Would that be OK?'

She put the measuring device on one of his fingers.

'Your oxygen is pretty low, Tom,' said Helen. 'You'll know what that means since you were a physician yourself. The lack of oxygen might be making you confused. I'd like to give you oxygen through these nasal cannulas. Would that be OK?'

Thomas closed his eyes. He could hear nothing now over the hissing of the oxygen in the tubes.

He wasn't enjoying at all being a patient in this hospital where he had been a consultant for many years. He had won a good reputation for himself as an excellent physician but, since retiring, his colleagues had seldom come near him. He had become lonely.

Then, six months ago, he had started to cough. The blood appeared. When he looked at the X-ray of his own lungs, he wasn't surprised. He already knew the name of his disease. He didn't have much time left.

The hissing of the oxygen was putting him off to sleep...

The doctors and medical students were doing a ward round, but I could see nothing but a wall of backs wearing white coats. Why were they being so disrespectful to me? I was the senior physician in charge of this department.

How ill-mannered! I turned on my heel and made for the main door of the ward.

On the other side of the door, I took a path that was going down through a pine wood.

As I was scrambling down the slope, I noticed a sound like thunder, or the rushing of water, growing louder and louder.

It didn't take long for me to reach the edge of the wood, where I found myself standing on a steep cliff high above a great roaring river.

That was when I saw the bridge.

It was a suspension bridge over the river. There was room on the footpath for only one pedestrian and, to make matters even more alarming, a fair number of the planks were missing. It was the kind of bridge you might see in a fantasy film.

Despite that, something was pulling me, drawing me to the bridge. I knew that I would have to go across it.

I was fearful when I put my right foot on the first plank, although it proved to be reliable enough. But I looked ahead of myself and that was a big mistake. I saw a man falling from the arch of the bridge, his arms beating the air like useless wings. He disappeared from sight in the deep river. If he screamed, I didn't hear it.

After that I kept my eyes on the walkway and went on

forwards, my heart thumping.

At the top of the arch, I almost fell off the bridge, I was so dizzy. My legs were shaking. I held on so tightly to the hand-rope that I thought my muscles were going to explode.

But I reached the other side and put my feet onto solid ground.

As I was getting my breath back, I noticed that there was a large house on the horizon. I set off on the path towards it.

The front door of the house was open, and I walked down a corridor and into a spacious room where a large crowd of people were chatting. It looked as if there was about to be a banquet.

It occurred to me that most of the people present in the room looked vaguely familiar, but it gave me a surprise when I saw my own father among them. He waved to me.

I was walking towards my father, feeling very happy, when I heard a sound like a cup clinking on a saucer – I turned my back on it.

In ward 5B, a young woman had come to offer a cup of tea to the patients.

'Would you like a cup of tea, Tom?' she asked.

'Tom?'

A Concert for Kwame
Sam Elder

The bell was delayed by ten meenits because the snaw had drapped heavier than expected. Thankfully, it wisnae ma turn tae bring in the lines; turn your back oan the wee cherubs oot there an ye were askin for a snowbaw aimed at your heid. Corridor duty wis bad enough that mornin, the pupils breengin in wae their ower-excited voices stoatin aff the bare brick wa's.

'Let it snaw, let it snaw, let it snaw,' I thocht. This was ma best day of the week, and I would enjoy it: a double period of the Highers before the interval, a promising second-year class, a non-contact period, twa wee first-year classes efter lunch, then hame before the roads froze up.

Come the interval, the snaw was getting deeper and the weans mair hysterical. Then in came ma second years – boisterous, drookit and burstin tae tell me something: 'Sur! Sur! Please, Sur!'

'Wait a minute,' I ordered. 'Sit doon and calm doon.' And they did. 'Now, hands up please – Joe, you go furst.'

'Sur, this is the furst time Kwame has seen snaw – EVER!'

Kwame was fairly new tae the class. A pupil in the school for nearly a year, he was wan of the asylum seekers welcomed tae the city jist before the millennium. Efter a spell in the English as a Second Language unit, he was being gradually introduced tae the wider curriculum. Polite but subdued in class, he struggled tae keep up wae the ithers when they were singing, and I was concerned that – understandably – he might be lonely. But I saw a different Kwame when he came in fae the snaw that day: he was grinnin fae lug tae lug! By now the class was becoming a free-for-all:

'Aa showed him how tae catch snowflakes in yur haun an watch them melt.'

'Aa telt him that every snowflake is different.'

'We showed him how tae make snowbaws.'

'Aa telt him that makin snowbaws is easier when ye wear gloves.'

I had tae raise ma voice again. 'Thank you, class! I've learned a few things masell there,' I said in a tone that indicated 'discussion over'.

I had planned a lesson oan major, minor and pentatonic scales, but assessing the situation, I hesitated. The troops were never slow tae pick up oan this, and sure enough, wan of the girls raised her haun and asked, 'Sur, can we sing?' That request was aye hard tae resist, and I gave in – but pretending I was da'en the class a big favour.

'OK,' I said slowly, trying tae think of a song in a minor key that might address ma topic, but before I got there, wan of the boys reminded me that they had learned 'The Snowman' before Christmas. That was in a minor key, so I persuaded massell that I was justified in lettin them perform it. Sorted!

The arrangement I used involved everybody: singers, glocks, keyboards, bass and acoustic guitars. It would take ten meenits tae set up the room, but the kids were weel drilled, and by the time I had designated the performers, got the parts oot the cupboard and haunded them roon, we were ready for a run-through. Then wan of the boys mentioned that Kwame widnae ken the song because he didnae jine the class till efter Christmas, and anither suggested, 'Sur, mebbe he could be the audience?' Before I could intervene, Kwame – slightly bamboozled – had been seated like a wee prince in front of the performance area.

Expectin the weans tae be a bit rusty, I went through the instrumental parts wan at a time, reminding them of the foutery key changes in the middle eight, then waarmed up the singers and reminded them tae watch their speed: 'The wee boy and the snowman in the film were floating in the clouds, no runnin for a bus,' I telt them. Finally, I clapped ma hauns three times and we were guid tae go.

I played the opening arpeggios on the piano tae set the tempo, then the glocks, keyboard and guitars played the melody through wance before the singers came in:

'We're walking in the air…'

It was a special moment for the class. Singing and playing before an audience creates a sense of occasion, and I could sense that the weans were making an effort tae impress their 'guest'. And they sailed through it! Efter the last few notes had floated away, there was a hush, and every heid turned tae Kwame. The boy looked flummoxed, but soon smiled and said, quietly, 'Beautiful.' And the performers let oot wan big, collective sigh.

At some point in whit was left of the period, I would have waffled oan aboot minor keys, the instruments would have been put away, the parts collected in and the class dismissed. But it wisnae as easy tae dismiss that lesson fae my mind; like a guid tune, it steyed wae me for the rest of the day.

When the final bell had rung and I was driving hame, I passed a bunch of weans building a snowman, and thocht again aboot ma second years and the 'beautiful' Snowman they had created thegither that mornin. It wis then, when I had time tae think aboot it, that I felt a surge of pride in ma pupils, remembering how they had looked efter Kwame in the playground, reassured him aboot the snaw and shown him how it could be fun. But mair than that, I was impressed wae how they had brocht their goodwill intae the classroom, and how keen they were tae share their music wae him; wae their innocent acts of kindness towards Kwame, they had made him feel part of the class.

Mebbe nane of this would have happened if it hadnae been for the weather, but I knew that Kwame's new freens would still be there for him long efter the snaw had meltit.

Author note: *Kwame's name has been chinged in the interests of privacy, but I still remember him and his class every time I hear that song, and whenever the snaw returns tae work its magic. . .*

Share your love of books. . .

Scottish Book Trust is an independent national charity. Our mission is to ensure people living in Scotland have equal access to books.

If you're enjoying this book, please consider making a donation so that everyone in Scotland has the opportunity to improve their life chances through books and the fundamental skills of reading and writing.

Visit **scottishbooktrust.com/donate** to find out more.

Friends we found in
difficult moments

The Lavender Letters
Manoshi Roy

It all began in the summer of 2004. My company
had sent me and another delegate to attend a two-
day conference in Zurich. Our return flights were on
different days – his was a day earlier, and mine was
nineteen hours later.

It was my first time travelling abroad, and I was
already anxious. When I learned about the return plan,
I took a deep breath and tried to stay composed. But
things took a turn at the airport: my flight was cancelled,
and the next one was sixteen hours later.

Though I was twenty-three, I'd lived a fairly sheltered
life. With my senior colleague already gone and no
idea how to navigate an international airport, I felt
overwhelmed. I sat on a bench, clutching my handbag,
trying not to cry. My international SIM had stopped
working – using foreign SIMs wasn't exactly smooth
back then.

That's when I noticed someone approaching.

'Hi, need help?' a stranger asked in broken English.

Tears welled up as I looked up to see a kind-faced
young woman gazing at me. I told her what had
happened.

She sat beside me and said, 'I know this is a difficult
situation, and you have every right to cry – but why
not turn it into a good experience? Come, let's fix your
problem.'

With that, she pulled me up and led me to the ticket
counter. In broken English, she firmly enquired about
my flight. Within minutes, she not only sorted out the
details and got me my boarding pass in advance but also

managed to secure a free lounge pass, still speaking in fragmented but confident English. I was amazed by her boldness and composure.

Once we settled in the lounge, she introduced herself as Luna, from Barcelona, Spain. She loved to solo travel to budget-friendly destinations – Zurich was her third. She worked as a front-desk executive and bartended on weekends. I shared a brief intro, too. Unable to pronounce my name, she affectionately called me Bonita.

With no common language beyond scattered English and excessive hand gestures, we wandered around the airport countless times for five unforgettable hours until it was time for her flight. She was a spirited and talkative girl with a hidden talent for empathy. Before leaving, she pulled out a lavender-coloured notepad, scribbled her home address on the first page, and added a note:

If you remember this day even once a year, write to me.

The letters begin

I kept my promise.

My first letter was simple – a thank you, a bit of office gossip, some weather talk, and a small, dried flower from my garden.

Luna replied two months later. Like her, her letter was full of life – stories about her extended family, the scent of spring in the air, a new dress, and a lost shoe. It was filled with spelling mistakes and grammatical errors, but it carried a charm that made me smile the entire time I read it.

That was the beginning of a friendship that lasted for years.

We never met again, never spoke on the phone, never emailed. We chose letters – slow, thoughtful, full of everyday stories – always written on lavender letter pads, something Luna insisted on.

Over time, our letters came regularly – four times a year, sometimes more.

In one, Luna dreamt of opening a flower shop filled with every colour and fragrance. In another, she shared how a cousin had landed a great job thanks to her advanced education – now, Luna wanted to return to her studies too.

Family, work and life moving on

Over time, life changed around us. I got married, had kids and juggled work, while Luna remained single, pursued her education and eventually landed a high-paying job.

My letters were filled with everyday things – pollution, fresh bread, school updates and office monotony. Her letters painted a vibrant picture of solo trips, a carefree spirit and her beloved cat.

Once, I mentioned my long-held dream of doing a PhD, but said time and money didn't allow it. Her reply was brief but firm: 'You've got one life. Chase your dreams.' The rest of the letter was about a charming doctor she seemed smitten with. I was happy for her.

Then, no reply to my next letter. It was unlike her, but I assumed she was caught up in a new romance.

Eventually, the letters resumed – but the doctor was never mentioned again.

As my life grew busier, I struggled to keep up with letter-writing, though I still managed one for every two of hers.

Then, in June 2016, her letters stopped completely. I had no phone number or email to reach her. I waited, worried.

In February 2018, a parcel arrived with international postage. Inside was a beautiful diary, a pen and a letter from Luna's sister, along with a generous cheque.

Luna had been diagnosed with stage 3 breast cancer and was undergoing chemotherapy. Too weak to write, she had asked her sister to send the gift. On the first page of the diary, in Luna's handwriting, were the words:

You've got one life. Don't just chase your dreams – grab hold of them. Apply for that PhD. Here's my little contribution.

That day, I cried like a child.

I later got her phone number and email from her sister and stayed in touch until her final days. In 2020, she contracted Covid, and her frail body couldn't survive the blow.

The final letter

A week after her passing, I received an email with an attachment – a photo she had taken of us at the airport years ago, both laughing uncontrollably. Below it, in her handwriting, were the words:

Always remember – you can laugh like this.

Then Again
Chitra Ramaswamy

1. Midlife isn't the easiest time to make new friends, nor sustain the old ones. Sometimes I am more lonely than a writer dare admit, striding the streets of my present, holding one of my children's sweet hands, dependable as the incoming dusk, carrying the bags and the keys and the time and the solutions and the blame, knowing where we are going, and how long it will take, pointing out the daisies shutting up shop for the night, forecasting the rainbow, while all the while I am elsewhere, back in the perpetual summer of my childhood, knocking on the doors of my childhood, waiting for the friends of my childhood to come out to play on the streets of my childhood, beneath the high noon sun of my childhood, until the mother of my childhood – dead now, almost five years – appears at the door, backlit by the past, wiping her hands on her sari, to call us in for dinner.

2. Then again, what of the Indian woman who sat next to me at the Julia Donaldson event in Edinburgh two years ago? Same age as me, though paler, Bengali my father would instantly note, as he did right then and there in my head, where the voices of my parents reside congenially alongside those of my friends, keeping me company in this more solitary stage of life. I was with my daughter, clutching the mouse who outsmarted the Gruffalo, she with her nephew holding – sorry, I can't recall. As the stories were told and the songs were sung and the babies were bounced on the knees of the determined mothers, first words were gingerly passed

back and forth between two middle-aged Indian women in the language reserved for strangers with shared undocumented histories. Afterwards she was the brave one who contacted me on Instagram. 'If you ever fancy going for a walk with a fellow brown woman...' On Portobello beach our similar hands made shy swirls in the sand as we shared stories the way girls swapped Garbage Pail cards in the playgrounds of my childhood. Then we went for another walk in Leith and talked about our dead mothers and our same-age fathers softening with age. Then we went for noodles. Now we are friends.

3. Then again, sometimes life will happen and I will want to mark it with a friend, and no face will materialise to inhabit that sacred noun. And I will scroll through my contacts, and start writing half-hearted messages on WhatsApp, and a mist of dissatisfaction will descend, bringing with it the desire to run which comes for all middle-aged people, now and then, squeezed as we perpetually are between the past and future of our too-set lives, until the blessed demands of that too-set life intervene to chivvy all that into the past, and I will forget that I needed a friend, because the children need me to put them to bed, and I'm dropping by 9pm anyway, and solitude is an old pair of pyjamas – nothing easier to put on.

4. Then again, what could I possibly have to complain about? I'm a restaurant critic! Every week I eat out somewhere different in Scotland, scouring the land through its menus, eating the story this country tells itself through its food, answering again and again the most gleeful question of them all, the one that never gets old – what can I get you? Meanwhile, opposite me

sit a cavalcade of friends old, new or in the process of being made. We eat and drink and talk, but nothing is recorded of that last part. My reviews are a record of the food, service, atmosphere and history. But what of the words digested with my friends? Where do they go?

5. Then again, what is a friend if not a partner with whom you've been through two births, three deaths, two books, various essays, two mortgages, half a dozen job changes, two rescue dogs, however-many Sunday night period dramas and viewings of *Carol*, and all the breakfasts, lunches and dinners I've cooked in love and haste, and the trips home to London, and the kitchen discos, and the most devastating arguments, and the biggest laughs over the smallest things, and the private language only we speak, learned over twenty years of what I too easily forget is friendship too.

6. Then again, after my mother died it was my oldest friends, the ones who knew her from the start, whom I yearned for most. I needed the proof only old friends can provide that her life mattered, that mine matters, that any of it happened at all. Recently my oldest friend and I sat on a bench while our four children played in the park around us, and she told me about her mother falling ill with what has turned out to be three different forms of late-stage cancer, and we were at once two terrified mothers and two little girls hurtling down the hills of our childhood on our bikes, and I told her that since my mother's death I have had no choice but to walk through a door into the second room of my life, and that room, though my own children, partner and precious life are contained in it, is so cold and unfurnished, and often I want only to retreat backwards like a spooked puppy,

shut the door for good, and we held hands, and would have wept if it hadn't been for a disaster involving my son and her daughter and a soft toy thrown over a wall onto a train track and so we leapt up out of our anguish to sort out the mess made by the next generation, and the conversation was left there hanging, like a lost hat on a fence, until we could return to pick it up once more. And that's what the best of friendships are – a conversation that never ends.

7. Then again, I have barely seen her over the last two decades, which is half the time we've known each other.

8. Then again, friendship is the memory that lives outside you, the history kept by a separate consciousness in time.

9. Then again, I miss my friends, which is another way to say I miss life's first act, the way there were more friends then as there was more future, and all those I loved were alive and well. Who knows where the time goes?

10. Then again, who knows what friends the future holds?

Me Pal an the Pairk
Josie Giles

Awa back in January 2021 – comin on a year o pandemic, anither lockdoun, me runnin smack bang intae anither burnoot eftir months o owerdaein hid wi mutual aid wark – I posted a peedie wird tae me trans community group chat. 'A'm no gettin mesel oot the hoose. Wid onybdy meet up wi me fer a weekly daunder aboot the pairk?' I got a reply fae somebdy A'd no met afore, anither trans wumman at bade up the road. Sheu sayed sheu'd come an fetch me, an sheu did. Sheu nivver missed a week, an even eftir I wis back tae mesel an takkin me ain body oot, we kept on meetin up tae staver an blether. The ae path, the ae pairk, but watchin hid cheenge as spring cam in.

Hid's Lochend Pairk, fifteen minutes up the bike path fae me road, a royetie bit o gress, trees an watter aneath the bruckalation o a auld tour hoose. Wi Duddingston, hid's wan o the twa natural lochs in Edinburgh, tho natural's a misnomer. The watter's a fair piece lower as it wance wis, an i' the fifties the city mad a boorach an plunkit buildin grummel i' the mids. They planted a few howpfu trees at sank and deed, makkan a oorie suckamire at's a perfect hame fer watter birds. Moss deuks an tappit deuks, Canada geese an stibble geese, snyths an swans – aw raiglar visitors, alang wi the resident huidie maws an rattons. Thir skrankie birks an bunnet firs fer passerines an squirrels. Hid taks us ten minutes tae gang aw the wey aroond, which we dae wance a week. Ivry time, we try tae spy the hegrie, Lang Sandy, a dowlie bird at's flitten fae the muckle nestin grund at Duddingston tae mak a hame in Lochend.

Aroond an aroond we gang, watchin the deuklins growe up an the cygnets hide in their mither's wings. We speak aboot boyfriend bither, the latest guff in the news, hou tae get whit we need fae wir doctors. The birks gang green, then gowd, then drap their leafs tae leave they slinkit brainches at purpie the winter. Me pal hits a winter wae, an nou hid's me turn tae drop by tae pick her up, get her oot, mak bad jokes, watch the few birds left coorie doon. The pairk's mad pals o us, an wir mad pals o the park. Whit stairted wi a favour is sunk in deeper, like the trees sinkin intae the loch, growin on grummel, makkan a safe piece fer sleek-feathered craiturs.

A year turns, an anither year. June 2023, an the virus is still wi wis, fer aw we mak oot itherweys, an the vyces in Pairlament is ivver mair ill. I gang fer surgery, an eftir a week o bed rest I've a need o folk tae help me oot the front door again. Me pal comes, reglar as ivver. A'm stechie, stentit an stoondit, no sure on me feet, no sure o me body. Hid's sair whan sheu gars me laugh. We bide a while on the bench. Lang Sandy's a mate nou: no so lanesome eftir aw. Sheu staunds i' the watter in that statue pose, a scuther o wind fufflan her lang chest feathers, watchin wis watchin her. Me pal delivers me hame an I gang back tae the sofa tae load up the Switch I've the lend o fer me recovery. I climb up a digital ben in Hyrule an watch the colours o the sunrise.

We're in a lot o group chats, me an me pal: fowk we swim wi, folk sheu's oot fer noodles wi, folk I pley boardgames wi. Wir seen mair as wan political organisin group come an gang thegither, brakkan under birnoot an bad relationship decisions. Thir a chart wi mak, like that wan i' *The L Word*, but fer trans weeman lukkan oot fer ilk ither. Each o wis is gotten a few girls we keep a ee on, each o thaim wi a few girls o their ain, an aw o wis tryan tae mak sure awbdy's catched somepiece i' the net. Whan the ae knot frays, anither's tied. Me an me pal, tho, wir fankelt thegither by this path: we loop the loch an it leashes wis.

By April 2025, the hegries is multiplied. A'm coonted seven, but Best kens hou mony is hidin. The swans is mense an pouer yet, an the snythlins are still gotten ridiculous feet, but the hegries ken they're the starns. Some glaikit beuys pit fire tae a bin on wir brand new observation deck, an the temporary crash barriers leuk like they'll be here tae stey. The birks is buddin. Me pal's awa fer surgery. Last week, tae see her aff, we daundered aroond the pairk an skrekkit aboot the latest aafil thing tae happen tae wir freends. The hegries didno mind. Next week, sheu'll be back, an we've a rota of pals tae come by and spend time wi her while sheu sits in bed an pleys videogames. Whan sheu's ready, A'll tak her oot, an we'll walk the path again.

Journey
Open Book Spinal Injuries Creative Writing Group
By Annie, Barrie and Bridget

He felt he'd been the grey man
while I sailed the high seas.
Unsettled – my anchor pulled adrift.

We parted because the tide turned, the wind blew,
we drifted – on different waves, on different seas,
in different ways.

I forgot, without intention,
our castles and our footprints in the sand.

Years had blessed and hurt us both.
Now each, as an old man, sees the other as a warrior.
We revel in tadpoles and baggy minnows – still little
boys.

Somewhere, deeply layered beneath all that life expected
we emerge from wrinkly cocoons and fly
like Superman again.

Unexpectedly
Philippa Ramsden

We never actually met.

I never saw her face
or heard her voice.
We bumped into each other
in this virtual world
became firm stranger-friends
unexpectedly,
bound together by a common
uninvited disease
invading, consuming our bodies,
too long undiscovered,
undisturbed.

Sharing tears
of laughter and darkest fear,
details deeply private
of degrading side effects,
scarring of mind and body, yet
each other's face, name
unknown, unfamiliar.

Holding each other's hands
we were pushed along
our medical paths,
disease and medications, trying,
but unable,
to strip us of dignity.

And one day

she was gone.

Stolen.
Abruptly.
Unexpectedly.

From her family.
From her friends.

And from a woman
she never actually met.

Author note: *When I was living and working in Myanmar, I was diagnosed with breast cancer. Treatment in Bangkok took nearly a year and, far from home in Scotland, I felt very isolated. Writing my blog enabled me to process the diagnosis and gruelling treatment path and particularly connected me with a community of people on similar paths. I became close with one woman even though I didn't know her name, only her blog name. Her diagnosis was terminal but her warmth, strength and personality shone through, hiding the severity of her illness. So I was completely taken by surprise when her husband announced her passing. I was utterly bereft, astounded that such a firm friendship could form when our connection was solely online. I wrote this poem to honour our friendship.*

Share your love of books. . .

Scottish Book Trust is an independent national charity. Our mission is to ensure people living in Scotland have equal access to books.

If you're enjoying this book, please consider making a donation so that everyone in Scotland has the opportunity to improve their life chances through books and the fundamental skills of reading and writing.

Visit **scottishbooktrust.com/donate** to find out more.

5O Word Non-Fiction

This is the second year we've run **50 Word Non-Fiction** as part of Scotland's Stories. We asked the public to share their true tales of Friendship in fifty words or fewer, using the premise of our popular monthly writing competition, 50 Word Fiction. This spin-off version proved popular once again, and we're delighted to showcase a selection of these super-short stories as part of this collection.

Sarah Cornelius

Melting mango ice drips down the sides of their cones. They sit on the grass sharing stories and untangling mixed-up memories. There are ripples of laughter, sprinkles of joy. No distractions, no distance, nowhere else to be. No pressure, no judgement, just patience and understanding. Best friends are forever treats.

Susan Ross

After thirty years of friendship, we expected prosecco on the patio. Instead, a shoulder-height pallet of lawn turf greeted us. Baking in the sun. Not good.

'I hope you don't mind,' she said. 'He won't help.'

Seven sweaty hours later, three bone-weary and contented gardeners popped a cork.

AW Wang

'Are you Cal's mum?' Your words warmly reached out, yet I with the quizzical brow questioned your approach.

'Cal has been so kind to Anders.' It was your son's first day at school. He hardly spoke any English.

I was humbled. Thankful. This was the beginning of our precious friendship.

Donna McCubbin

Every time I stepped into the garden, a little bell chimed hello. She leapt the wall, appearing beside me as I read, weeded or hung washing. We shared sunshine, watched butterflies, enjoyed quiet companionship. Then the moving vans came. The beautiful memories stay. I still longingly listen for her bell.

Eleanor Fordyce

Maureen and sister Nora each had a precious tin containing a week's sixpence-worth of sweets – aniseed balls, Parma Violets, jelly beans. I had no such tin but without debate, they took it in turn to allow me to sample their revered contents – a shared treat, never forgotten.

Barrie Baker

Lit by a full moon one August, I wandered anticlockwise around the park. Lost in painful memory of days long gone. She came clockwise, gazing at the moon. We spoke at once. Older souls past hesitating. We walked on together, clockwise, we still do. Friendship found, living rewound.

Greta Yorke

Friends are comfy slippers.
They're that cosy cardi
that soothes and warms
the chilled or aching being.
In their company you're you,
no façade,
no point.
Through years of contact,
brief, perhaps infrequent,
they're as they were yesterday
with all that shared experience,
wonderful years of discovery
together.
Treasure friends.

Morag MacDonald

I'm recovering from a really bad case of…
haircut.
I look like Beaker from *The Muppets* when I wake up
and Rod Stewart after I beat the haircut into submission.
In windy conditions it's all a bit Queen Camilla…
but only on one side.
My friend said, 'It'll grow back.'

Elizabeth Hepburn

'I've makit ower much soup, cuid ye yaise it?'
    We baith ken. Kid oan we dinnae.
    'Guid o ye.'

'Nae loss whit a freen gets.'

It's a sair fecht. Hungry bairns an nae siller. The faither's wages gae tae the pub.

He wid drink it thru a durty cloot.

Felix Pawlyn

I stared at them as we lay in bed. If anyone had seen us, speculation would have burnt through the room and spread down the street out into the city, reducing it all to ash. A presumption on limitations of love – that love of this strength was reserved for lovers.

Helen Harradine

You were my oldest. My steadfast. The one that I thought would always be around, but then you disappeared – vanished – and became vacant from my life. There has been a slow realisation that maybe you meant more to me than I to you, but still, there is an immense tenderness.

Hunter McAuley

1980s Dundee. Paul. Wit, raconteur, DJ, cartoonist and fellow student. Sharp as a tack, clever, good-looking, girls loved him. What's not to envy? Was fae Edinburgh, ken?

Got me into AC/DC, Eagles, Supertramp. We eventually lost touch. Hope you're going well, mate. Wish we had mobiles and Facebook then!

Jacqueline Munro

'You're my best friend, d'ya know that?'

Your baby blues stare into my own. You've never known anything else. Before you could comprehend the sun rise, the flow of air to your lungs, before you even understood there was a you… you knew there was me. Your best friend.

Laura Cooney

She makes me toast.
The kind after a baby comes.
But it's me being reborn at her kitchen table.
Examining myself. My head, a red light, my heart, viridian.
She's in full support of my fucked-up traffic lights.
'It's fine.
So long as there's bread, butter,
me. It doesn't matter which you choose.'

Bella Ball

A lifetime later I learned we shared something more profound than having started school together.

With memories of our laughter still fresh, I know we found a solace that carried us through the darkest of times, surviving abusive parents.

It was a friendship that taught me love. Thank you, my friend.

Lauren Beasley

There's a cyber-attack. Supermarket shelves are empty. Our little community shop still has food. I'm a shop assistant and I'm overwhelmed. I feel like crying. My friend comes in and buys an ice cream. I scan it and give it to her. 'No,' she says. 'It's for you.'

Simon Thoumire

Christmas 1982: I unwrapped a bagpipe chanter. Disappointed, I told classmates I'd gotten clothes.

Forty years later, my fingers feel their way across the same wooden companion, composing new music to be performed at Piping Live. The gift I never wanted became the friend I never knew I needed.

Duncan Carmichael

'Dave's had a heart attack. I'm at the hospital.'

'Christ – he's only thirty-one! What are the doctors saying?'

'That he was lucky we called the ambulance when we did. He looks fine now.'

'Jeez. Is it too early to start rippin the piss out of him?'

'I've already started.'

Share your love of books. . .

Scottish Book Trust is an independent national charity. Our mission is to ensure people living in Scotland have equal access to books.

If you're enjoying this book, please consider making a donation so that everyone in Scotland has the opportunity to improve their life chances through books and the fundamental skills of reading and writing.

Visit **scottishbooktrust.com/donate** to find out more.

Friends for life

My Letter to Him
Bamidele Bamgbopa

Dear Gbenga,

I can't believe it has been five years since we last spoke. However, I am not worried, because I can always write letters to you, knowing fully well that whenever I see you, we will reconnect again.

Writing this letter is hard for me. Hard, because there are so many things I would like to tell you since we last spoke, but penning them down cannot be compared to saying them to you face to face. Despite this, I'll keep writing to you as many letters as I can. It is therapeutic for me as well as gladdening that you, my friend, are forever cherished. I wouldn't let the distance between us deter me.

Just some days ago, I was thinking about how we became friends. I remember how on the very first day we met, you were sizing me up even before you walked up to me to say 'hello'. It was the most unlikely place for friendship to blossom – a job interview. In retrospect, I can now laugh at us, but then, I wasn't the friendliest. Can you blame me? I came to get a job and not to meet a friend. It turned out that you made the first move, not minding my attitude. I'm happy you went ahead and spoke to me first. The first words were spoken by you, and we became friends gradually. Now, a friendship that has been through thick and thin.

Back in those days when our friendship started, it seemed to me that you were a gentleman who was 'too good to be true', only for me to find out, as time progressed, that you actually were not feigning it.

In such a big city like Lagos, I wasn't expecting to meet

a friend like you. A city, with all of its glitz, glamour and paparazzi, could have had you caught up in its mix, but you still decided to stand out till our paths crossed. You are such a rare gem.

Can you believe that I saved your name as *Mon Amie* on my phone? These French words mean 'my friend' in the English language. You, indeed, are the type of friend I am so happy that I crossed paths with. Who could have thought that the friendship was going to last this long?

How are you doing over there? (Pardon me, please. I should have asked this question at the start of the letter, but I guess I was caught up in reminiscing on how we became friends.)

Can you believe that since the last time we spoke, I have not met any other friend like you? I mean, there are other 'friends', but among them all, you are outstanding. I am not saying all of this in order to flatter you, but I would be doing you a disservice if I did not mention this truth. Thank you for being that friend!

Guess what my new name is? I mean the new alias that comes behind my first name – a widow.

I am now being called a widow because you, my dear friend, Gbenga, departed. The whole world assumes that our friendship ended when you left. Little do they know that we are still friends. Friends for life!

They say I am living in denial, but would that really be true when you gave me gifts – our children, who are constant reminders of our friendship that I hold so dear.

Whenever I look at the children that our friendship produced, I cannot help but cheer up. These children embody your values, principles and even some of your physical features.

Your daughter has countlessly asked me how we became friends. She has seen your photos, your diary, and videos of you saved on my phone. Your son is quieter. He reminds me of you a lot. He talks very softly, like you.

Can you remember how you always told me that I could achieve great feats? You had a way of bringing out the best in me. Little wonder our friendship has thrived. Who better to be friends with, if not someone like you, whose words make me stretch myself beyond my comfort zone?

I have travelled to places, taken more educational courses, charted a new career path, and most of all, I'm raising our children all by myself.

Sincerely, being a widowed, single mom isn't easy. I can go on and on about the challenges and difficulties, but knowing fully well that I'm doing this for the sake of our friendship and knowing that you would have done the same for me if you were in my shoes, has been my major driving force.

I hope you are so proud of me!

Yours in friendship,
Bamidele

Author note: *This is a real letter written to my friend and late husband. Reminiscing on how strong the friendship we shared was, is what inspired my story. I hope this letter helps other widows and widowers write this type of letter to their departed loved ones. For some, it could even start the process of their healing.*

Heather
KM Black

Wi Heather, I find my fit,
A sense o belangin, a familiar face yet,
Years o memories, laughter, and tears,
A bond that's strong, through aa the years.

We dinnae need words, we jist ken,
A glance, a nod, a knowin hand, ye ken?
In a world that's loud and wide,
Our friendship's a safe, quiet tide.

Ye get me, Heather, in a way that's rare,
Nae judgments, nae expectations tae share,
Jist acceptance, and a heart that's true,
A friend whae's been there, through and through.

We look back on auld times and smile,
Shared moments, forever worthwhile,
The laughter, the fun, the memories we've made,
Moments that bring us tae oor knees wi joy displayed.

But it's mair than jist the memories we hae,
It's the feelin o bein understood, o bein bold,
In yer company, I am masel,
Free tae be autistic, wild, and carefree.

I hope I'm there for ye, in quiet ways,
A steady presence, through life's ups and downs, each
day,
A listenin lug, a helpin hand,
A friend whae's tryin tae understand.

Wi Heather, I find my voice,
A sense o self, a heartfelt choice,
Tae be masel, wi'oot apology or fear,
A gift that's precious, and oh sae dear.

Author note: *I'm autistic and have found it hard to make and keep friends over the years but with my friend Heather I don't feel autistic or awkward or weird. It's just such a pleasure to be myself without trying.*

Tai Chi and Hot Chocolate
Joanne Maybury

Each time I visit now you are weaker, smaller. Your
clothes hang. You are melting like a winter ice sculpture.
I hug you and joke that I can count your ribs. (They are
all still there.) Last week we sat, as is our new habit, in
your sitting room facing each other. You still felt well
enough to stand proud for me when I entered the room.
We talked about economics, doctors' appointments,
pain relief and bonsai trees. We tried to work out how
long we had known one another and settled on around
a dozen years. We watched two roe deer pass under the
trees on the other side of the river.

Today you have disappeared a little more, and with
your ravaged flesh comes your morphine-dulled mind.
I sit listening to the district nurse and notice your
mountaineer's hands. They still look capable. Look
overlarge against your collapsing chest. They flutter like
eagles' pinions in the high thermals.

We met at a tai chi class and, both being new, kept one
another company at the end of the back row. We made
comments under our breath to one another during the
routines and sometimes got told off. We'd keep one
another straight while we learnt the challenging moves
of The Fan. I'd show off my Parting the Horse's Mane.
Then there came a diagnosis and the tai chi ladies rally
round. I visit you in hospital and get catheter tales, and
later we welcome you back to your place. I'd missed you
at my back.

We stop tai chi but promise to keep meeting. You tell
me the best place in town for hot chocolate so that is
where we meet, every other Monday morning. I don't

tell you I'm not that bothered about hot chocolate. Ten years of drinking hot chocolate for you. We perch in the window seat and you carefully sprinkle brown sugar on the foam and watch it slowly sink. The first sip, and you smack your lips in appreciation. We talk about the state of the country, Nicola, wind farms, the Common Riding, your latest favourite recipe, our children. You talk about mountaineering, trips to the Himalayas, your birds of prey, and I talk about living in Uganda. You tell me about the bent copper in your division and the philandering sergeant, that you hated having to turn out for the miners' strikes. I tell you I write poetry and you look worried, but you like some a lot. Somehow we drink our way through (is it four, or five?) prime ministers and a couple of presidents.

Then, one day, something they call Covid happens and we are locked away. I phone you because I know you will be getting more and more depressed and you will want to talk but won't be able to make the decision to call me. Then they let us outdoors and we meet up in the park. At New Year we huddle in the Chinese pavilion with coffee and rum and Christmas cake, yours with butter because, 'bad cake needs butter and good cake deserves butter'. Mine is good cake. We wonder if we'll be arrested for sitting together in public, like those people in England, and imagine the headline in the local paper about the ex-policeman and the elder of the Kirk. Later they let us meet indoors and we return to our café, fiddling with masks and signing in. We hug when we meet and hug when we say goodbye. In front of everyone. We don't care. We need a hug. 'Keep smiling,' you say. 'Keep breathing,' I say, and we wave each other off.

Months pass and a recurring theme becomes your 'numbers'. They are rising, slowly. Maybe the drugs aren't holding back the cancer anymore. We talk about what might come, about palliative and end-of-life care. You tell me to make you laugh. I try and sometimes succeed. Then something changes. You get an infection that knocks you sideways. You start losing weight and even more strength. We meet up a few times, then one Sunday afternoon you call me. You sound upbeat, and I go to your house.

You are ready for me. You have prepared. You put me on the sofa and sit opposite me, look into my face and take my hand. I can't remember what you said. Something about having been in hospital, that they were upfront with you (at last), there is nothing more to be done and that you are dying, but it's all right, now that you know what you suspected. I know it had to come, but I am not ready. I say we will keep meeting for as long as you want to. We will take our hot chocolates for as long as we can.

And now here I am, sitting on the side of your bed, holding your hand, telling you I won't stop coming, saying call me any time and I'll come even for just ten minutes, that I am praying for you. You nod and say thank you and I let you sleep.

When this is done, which will be sooner than we would like, but at the right time, I will choose a bonsai tree from your collection and learn to care for it. You particularly said I should take a juniper. I will browse your books and choose a few as you have asked. I will ask for your green hat. And I will go to our café one Monday morning and sit in the window. I will picture you there, dapper in your polished shoes, pressed shirt and silk cravat, a glinting diamond stud in your ear and a twinkle in your eyes. I will raise a mug of hot chocolate to you, take a sip and smack my lips.

Author note: *I knew my friend's death was close and suddenly I wanted to write something about our friendship and to show it to him, or read it to him, before he died. Unfortunately, he died just twelve hours after I'd written it and before I'd seen him again.*

Have You?
Glenn Merrilees

Have you ever had a friendship,
That blossomed into love,
Loneliness forgotten,
As you thank the stars above?

Have you ever whispered secrets,
Ones you never thought you'd share,
Had a friend who'd listen,
Had a friend who'd care?

Have you ever seen the beauty,
In a partner's childbirth pain,
Or felt her adoration,
While dancing in the rain?

Have you ever watched her sleeping,
As you gently stroked her skin,
Adoration in your fingertips,
A love from deep within?

Have you ever suffered heartache,
Being parted for a day,
Counting down the seconds,
You'd trade your soul away?

Have you ever separated,
And suffered monstrous pain,
Every fibre in your body,
Yearns to hold her once again?

Have you ever watched a thunderstorm,
In a lover's warm embrace,
Or caught a tear of happiness,
Running down her face?

Have you ever watched a sunset,
Then watched the stars above,
The bubble that you're living in,
A bubble filled with love?

Have you ever heard contentment,
In a lover's subtle sighs,
Two as one united,
As you lay between her thighs?

All these things, well I have done,
And oh so many more,
A lucky, lucky, lucky man,
With the lady I adore.

Author note: *I've written many for my partner Aileen over the years but this is her favourite one. We have been together thirty-four years.*

We Need Tae Get a Pint
Scott Ferguson

It's finally arrived, the pint.

The pint you'd both been threatening for how long
now? Six months? Nine months? It canny be that long,
surely?

Aye, actually, his wedding had been in summer last
year. That was nine months ago, this is the pint that
you'd so earnestly suggested. You'd held the big man
in your drunken arms, and with hot breath in his ear,
you'd spoken with ferocity. It was then that the pint had
transcended from suggestion to promise.

You'd left him out on the white gravel in front of the
hotel. His new wife beside him, the happiest he'd ever
been, waving off their guests as they'd boarded the buses
home.

You remembered your kilt swishing in the cool night
air as you'd left them and climbed on. One last wave
from the steps before you found a seat by the window
and rested your sweaty head against it. As merry songs
arose from pockets of the bus, you told yourself you'd
see him again soon.

The initial time proceeding the wedding was obviously
too soon for the pint, but those months were truly
the golden ones. Long nights, nicer weather, ample
opportunity and hours to grab the pint, or a walk, or
some dinner. You lived thirty minutes away, though, so
you convinced yourself it was too hard during the week.

He'd had his honeymoon; you'd had your own summer
holiday. And then? Work, weekends recovering from
work, weekends with other friends, weekends with
family, and finally, winter. No golden nights, no golden

pints.

But now, nine months on, on a golden night, you had one another. As you walked down to the pub in your hometown, you tried to swallow the small bout of anxiety that had crept up inside of you. You detested it. As a man of thirty-three, you were struggling to understand why you had grown to be like this. Subtly nervous about meeting someone you had known all your life. Someone who had already seen you naked, seen you cry, seen you in love, seen you lose it, seen you nutted.

When spending time with someone from your past, it was hard not to reflect on the person you used to be. Carefree and confident, you hadn't known what anxiety was. You'd heard of it, but it wasn't something that used to exhaust you en route to a pint with one of your mates. And yet, maybe that was just how adulthood was for most people, maybe it was just the human condition.

You opened the door of the pub to a euphony of chatter and laughter, and your body was flooded with warmth and cheerfulness. You looked towards the bar and recognised the sandy hair on the back of your best friend's head. A white polo shirt hugged his stout frame, and his gaze shifted from left to right as he scanned the beer taps.

You walked up to him and placed a firm hand on his shoulder. He turned around, and for the first time in months, you saw the big, happy face of one of your oldest friends. With an almighty smile, he wrapped his thick arms around you.

'My mannn!'

He planted a wet kiss on your cheek, and then, it was as it was always going to be.

He pulled away, held you at arm's length, and looked

you up and down.

'Fuck sake, you wearing that shirt for a bet?'

'Shut it,' you laughed, moving to twist one of his nipples.

He chuckled, and with the instincts of a teenager, raised his hand to brush yours away.

'Here!'

He slung an arm over your shoulder and spun you around. He pointed to the beer tap on the far right of the bar.

'Look what they've got back in!'

You looked across to see the royal blue badge of Fürstenberg Pilsner, the only German lager available on tap in the town. You ordered, but they were changing the keg; they would bring the pints over.

You wandered over to the alcove of the pub, and your old table was free. The place where you had sat years ago and spoken of girls, tales from school, your grand plans for each other, The Biff and fitba. Now? Your wives, tales from work, your grand plans for yourself, Fontaines DC and fitba. The beautiful game, and the team you support, is one of life's only constants.

Then came the beer. You both sat entranced as a beer mat, and then the pint, was placed down in front of you. The head was like whipped cream, a white crown atop the golden nectar. You clinked your glasses together and drank deeply, and never had you had a drink like it.

Your chat, as it usually did, soon found comfort and laughter in stories of 'do you remember?' Someone had once said that this was the lowest form of conversation, but you disagreed.

Few people burn brightly in your life from its beginning to its end; you should always cherish the times when they did. Talk of the times you saw one another naked, crying, in love, losing it, or nutted.

After, warmed by the cloak of a four-pint buzz, another promise was made.

'We'll try to get something sorted for next month.'

You knew this wouldn't be the case, but that was OK.

You embraced deeply, and with your world as settled as it could possibly be in that moment, both walked in opposite directions.

Author note: *I was working, and realised that I probably spent more time with clients and colleagues than I do with some of the people who make me the happiest. It made me miss my old friends, and the fact that so often quality time with them is squeezed into a bi-annual slot of a few pints.*

The Shoes
Ann Craig

It was 8.30 in the morning, I was filling the kettle when
my mobile phone rang. It was a pal, telling me they were
playing our song as she was driving to work, and she
just had to stop and sing along, so should I, and I should
dance too, wherever I was. Her voice sounded high,
desperate, with Gloria Gaynor belting out 'I Will Survive'
in the background.

'What's wrong, Maggie?'

'I've got cancer.'

Her voice sounded like a child's.

Tears fell at both ends of the phone as I heard the
details.

'OK,' I said. 'We can do this; it'll be a sore time but here
we go.'

She was a close friend, who stayed a distance away,
but our lives had always intertwined. We knew each
other well. I looked up potions and lotions to offset the
sickness. I tried to phone at times when I knew it would
be difficult, when she would need a friend, not family.
I reassured her when she wondered if the girls would
be OK. But it was the shoes that got us through the days
she was having the cure dripped into her and she was
scared.

When they made mistakes and she would text, 'Bloody
medical experts, better off with witch doctors!'

I would tell her to shout and scream and make a fuss,
which she never did. Then one day when her arm was
strapped and her movement restricted, she texted me a
photograph of her feet and the shoes she was wearing
that day. They were like cozy slipper boots, cuddling her

feet.

It became our thing. Her shoes became our secret, that told me how she was doing that day. We talked about them as we shared our big and little thoughts about living and dying.

Sometimes her shoes would be a shiny vivid red, and we would vent our anger about a world that allowed this disease to exist. Was it our fault? Were we poisoning the earth with our greed? Who could we blame?

Sometimes they would be white shoes with little blue bows, her feet pale and naked in them like two small bodies. We would reminisce about our youth, our children, when they were young, our hopes and fears for them. We would feel very small in a world made scary by our fears. Then once she showed me black shoes laced up tight, the kind you wore with black clothes, and I was scared to answer her text.

'What's up?'

She said, 'It's raining. You know Buddhists see existence like an empty cup that is bobbing on the river of life. Then we fill it with our experiences in this life, until it sinks back into the river again, only to bob up empty again ready for the next go. What do you think?'

I was careful when I answered. 'Personally I'd like to be a huge mug, but right now I'm acting like a saucer for your cup, so no spilling over just yet please.'

Death carefully tiptoed around in those clumpy black shoes.

The weeks wore on and the shoes became solid, sturdy, a determined look about them. She wore Doc Marten boots one day and I wondered who she would be kicking. Another day it was high wedge heels; very strappy, very sexy. There had been a great-looking doctor around the last few weeks on the ward. What else could she do to attract some attention?

Then one day instead of her feet, she showed me her arm and I cried at the sore sight of it. She said, 'No don't, it's just because this is the last one, then the op and then the home stretch.'

'OK, so get your running shoes on then,' and she panned down to her feet and there they were: shiny new Adidas all ready for the last lap.

The last photograph she sent showed her feet naked without shoes, exposed and raw looking, as she waited for the final results. Her toenails painted defiantly red with little targets on them. 'Scanxiety' a real thing in our stomachs.

When I saw her next, as we hugged our happiness and relief, I looked down and she had on the brightest pair of rainbow-coloured sandals I've ever seen. They were luminous and sparkled, not in any way sophisticated or stylish.

Then underneath, painted in multi coloured lettering across both shoes:

Sole survivors, soul sisters

She handed me an identical pair and it was time to dance to our song again, and we did.

Share your love of books. . .

Scottish Book Trust is an independent national charity. Our mission is to ensure people living in Scotland have equal access to books.

If you're enjoying this book, please consider making a donation so that everyone in Scotland has the opportunity to improve their life chances through books and the fundamental skills of reading and writing.

Visit **scottishbooktrust.com/donate** to find out more.

Unexpected friendships

Clarice, Queen of the Sun Inn
Catherine Simpson

Growing up on a dairy farm in Lancashire, the only terraced houses I was familiar with were on *Coronation Street* – until I was nineteen and got a job fifty miles away in a rundown northern mill town, and then I bought a *Coronation Street* house of my own. On the first night, alone, in my new 'two-up, two-down' there was a knock on the door.

'I'm Clarice, from next door,' said a lady with a white perm, 'and my man's Bob,' and she handed me a bottle of home-brew with a handwritten label: **Parsnip**.

Clarice was in her late sixties. Before I met her, my friends were all my own age, and I had never contemplated friendship with someone fifty years my senior.

Immediately Clarice took me under her wing. She started taking me down to her local, the Sun Inn, where she had her own spot at the end of the bar next to a man with an ill-fitting prosthetic face and another man with a false leg that he removed after several pints. Clarice, it seemed, baked meat and potato pies for half the pub regulars – the widowers, the very elderly and others who were semi-housebound – and would dish them out in battered cooking tins wrapped in tea towels.

Clarice was loud, outspoken and funny. She was five feet ten and never went out without her lipstick and her eyebrows.

Clarice was the Queen of the Sun Inn.

This was the early eighties, and one evening there was a meeting of the National Front in the back room of the Sun Inn. One skinhead in tight jeans and bovver boots swaggered past to peer through the window into the street. 'Ah, are you looking for your mummy?' said Clarice. 'Is she coming for you?' And she smiled at him insincerely until he sloped off.

Soon I was spending every Sunday evening in Clarice and Bob's front room watching Agatha Christie TV dramas while drinking gin and tonic and eating roast chicken sandwiches as the heat from the gas fire prickled our shins.

Everything seemed exotic at Clarice's. Even the gas fire, because there had been no gas in my home village, and until recently we'd had to rely on open fires. Gin and tonic was also new to me – before this, I had drunk gin sweetened with orange cordial.

In Clarice's over-furnished front room, surrounded by years of ornaments, cards and clutter, we would squeeze onto her sofa among her knitting bags and patterns, with her Siamese cat – Pinkie ('Mr Pinkerton' on a Sunday) – lying along the backrest. Sometimes, Clarice would put on a record, close her eyes, sink onto the sofa and sigh with delight at the sound of Mario Lanza singing 'My Heart Stood Still'. This was exotic too, especially as I thought the singer was someone called Marie O'Lanza. I mean, I already knew there was a male singer called Val, so why not?

Clarice loved people and their stories. She'd wait until Bob dozed off in his armchair before telling me what she'd got up to with her lover during the Second World War. She had been married to a different man back then, an invalid with heart disease who had taken to his bed in the living room soon after their only child was born. Clarice had been attached to the Canadian Army Pay Corp for the duration of the war in a town forty miles away, where her lover happened to have a shop. They would spend all week together as man and wife before returning the forty miles to their legal spouses at the weekend.

As we drank gin, she would root in the side-pocket of her handbag and take out a photograph of her lover – who looked like Ernest Hemingway in a greatcoat – and weep over it. She would tell me that even after her husband died, she could not marry her lover because his wife was a Catholic who would not agree to a divorce. When her lover died suddenly of a heart attack, Clarice could not go to the funeral for fear of the reception from his wife and family. As she recounted this bit, she would extract a hankie from the sleeve of her jumper and wipe her eyes.

Then she would show me another photograph taken at the same time – this one of herself, blowing a kiss towards the camera (or to her lover, who had taken it) as she posed in a velvet-collared, hound's-tooth suit nipped in at the waist. Studying that picture always cheered her up a bit, and she would declare: 'If I had my time again, Cath, I'd do everything twice as fast, twice as often and twice as reg'lar.'

She approved of the pencil skirts and high heels I wore for my office job, and that I religiously curled my hair with heated rollers and never left the house without full make-up. 'There's no point in having your stall set out and your blinds down, Cath.'

I got a boyfriend who had a sports car, and she approved of him too – despite my telling her that I knew he was not to be trusted. She would hover behind her net curtains as he drew up in his gold car, which was as long as her house, and watch him as he straightened his designer jacket and did up one of the buttons before knocking on my door.

Life was for living, said Clarice. Enjoy things while they lasted, she said, because nothing lasted forever. She knew that much.

'Think on, Cath,' she'd say, as Bob went to fetch the Gordon's bottle. 'Twice as fast, twice as often and twice as reg'lar.' And I'd clink my glass of gin against hers to raise a toast to my best friend, my neighbour, confidante, surrogate mother and mentor.

To Clarice, Queen of the Sun Inn.

4,152 Miles
Lorna Fraser

We don't write letters anymore.

It's been years since we've taken our pen to that onion skin airmail paper, the one that folded into itself. A defined space to fit all the words we had to share.

I would seal them up and post them through the letter box at the corner of the street. A short walk to send my thoughts flying through the air.

You had further to go to get your message to me. A drive into town in your dad's pickup truck, standing in line at the mailing office so you could hand it over. You lived in a small, wild place and everyone knew I was your friend.

Remember how it all started? Of course you do. Me too!

Though the precise date of our first communication has long since been lost, it's enough that we know we were twelve years old. Born the same year, a few months apart, and separated by 4,152 miles.

I was a Girl Guide in Scotland, and you were a Girl Guide in Canada. We had both applied to the Girl Guiding Pen Pal Scheme. Long since defunct, the scheme matched us together and so began our friendship.

I still have some of the letters you wrote. I don't quite know how the others were lost, for they were always too important to discard. I expect you are the same. Though nowadays you have far less space for possessions and it's of no matter if they have gone.

Our first letters were filled with the chatter of innocents. We shared the details of our lives, stories of family and school and Girl Guides, taking fascinated pleasure in how different our worlds were.

We were at an age when the novelty of a pen pal might soon wane, yet we kept going all through our school years. Sometimes the standard airmail letter was not enough so we wrote on sheets of thin paper, supplemented with photographs, packed into an envelope. You weren't the only one then who had to make a special trip to the post office to pay the correct mailing charge.

We had never once spoken aloud, yet our voices were clear. We knew each other, we understood each other, and we trusted each other. There was always something to write about.

At eighteen, I moved from the Fife town where I lived to go to university in Edinburgh. It was exciting and absorbing. Your life was changing too. While I was studying history you were getting married, having your first baby.

For a while, our letters were separated by time and space. People say that with a real friend, there can be periods when you do not or cannot get together but when you meet up after a month, a year, two years or more, you simply pick up where you left off. That was us. The only difference, our meetings were in words.

More years went by. We wrote, sometimes a lot, sometimes less so. We had never met and still our friendship endured.

I will never forget the first time I heard your voice.

You made the call across those four thousand miles from British Columbia to Scotland. My last letter to you had told of the loss of my brother, sharing the shock and the grief of it all. You knew instinctively that your words could not wait for a letter, because that's what a true friend does. They open their arms and their heart and hold, hold, hold on tight.

As I write this now, although I feel the prick of a painful memory, I find myself smiling at the ease and warmth of our conversation. It led to a plan which came to fruition two years later. We met! Face to face. We hugged, we laughed, we talked and talked, like old friends do.

I travelled with my husband from our Edinburgh city flat to your home, a log cabin house surrounded by woods and hills. We stayed with you, your husband and your two lovely boys and you took us on a Canadian adventure. Bear trails, salmon fishing, heritage and history, barbeques of hunted meats. Forests, lakes, rivers and mountains. I still have all the photos.

It was the trip of a lifetime, but for all the excitement, the best part was you and me. Two friends who naturally moulded together, in carefree chatter and comfortable silences.

That trip was twenty-nine years ago. Our lives have changed so much since then. How did we both become sixty years old? Will we ever meet face to face again?

You are still the wilderness girl, at home with the high peaks, the fast-flowing rivers and living simply with your beloved dog.

As for me, I moved, with my husband and our dog, from our urban life to the rural north-east of Scotland. Now we have our own mountain view.

We don't write letters anymore. We don't send photos in the post.

Instead, news of our lives is shared through the filter of social media. Pictures on Instagram, posts on Facebook, chats on WhatsApp. Still a card at Christmas though!

We don't write letters anymore, but that doesn't

matter.

This friendship, sown long ago with tentative, simple, seedling words, is forever connected by 4,152 miles of braided roots, tightly twisted, strong and unbreakable.

Author note: *I was inspired by one of my longest friendships which began with the words 'Dear Susan. . .' It seems apt to tell this true story of a friendship founded in letter writing and to write as if I were speaking directly to my dear friend.*

A Blizzard in a Teapot
Aileen MacAlister

It's late, maybe 10pm. I haven't been keeping the best time recently, with so much to think about. But I know it is after 9pm, because that is when I finished work.

I'm sitting in my car in the supermarket car park. It's dark, has been for hours. Winter in Scotland has to be the worst time to go through the death of a parent. A Scottish winter has the possibility to be the best and most welcoming, cosy time of year, with Christmas lights and fairytale pantomimes, comfort food and warming fires. Or, and for me in this moment, it is bleak and uncaring. Cold and full of dread.

The supermarket's neon glow is an assault. The thought of being bathed in its fake warmth, the loud music and chatting shoppers, busy even at this late hour as people prepare for the most wonderful time of the year, is immobilising. I am frozen in its hyper beam. Glued to the spot like a ribbon on a box.

I probably should have called in sick today; he's not gone yet but it won't be long, and it's hard enough to get up and moving, let alone be cheerful to customers all day. Serving hot coffee and cakes as people exchange gifts and pleasantries. How fun it is to listen to fifty different flocks of festive people have the same conversations all day, everyday.

Partially I am in denial that this is having any effect on me. I am fine, that is my go to response. So why, then, am I frozen in a supermarket car park? All I need is a carton of milk and something for breakfast.

Get out of the car, go buy what you need and then you can go home.

Nope, nothing. Cannot move. My mind has too many thoughts racing through it, I can't seem to catch one long enough to bring it into focus.

Try Gregor, he has a level head.

He might not be close by but he usually answers the phone when I call. He knows me well enough to strike the right balance of encouragement and practicality that could bring me out of whatever state it is that I have found myself in.

The call doesn't last long; he's just on his way out. Of course, I should have realised, it's a Friday night in December. But it works, to some extent. I'm not blaming myself for yesterday's misadventure any more and I have recovered some of my senses. I'm still stranded alone in the car park though. I need someone to physically drag me from this spot, to pull me round the supermarket and snap me out of this fog.

I pick up the phone again. Annie is a new friend, but she has the kind of personality that draws people to her. The kind of person that knows every regular by name and starts making their coffee before they even enter the shop. Can I burden her with this? Can I show my weakness to such a new presence in my life?

She's on her way. We are going to buy milk and something for breakfast and then, despite the late hour, we are going to have a cup of tea.

*

I am no longer frozen in place. We walk around the supermarket at a steady pace and pick up a few biscuits for good measure. I am still out of focus, but she provides stability as we wind our way through the aisles.

Back in the car park, we approach our cars. She checks

I'm OK to drive and then I follow the red lights of her car round the meandering country roads. Her house isn't far but it is outside town, a peaceful hidden world near the river mouth. During the day you can see the river and in summer her garden is full of life.

There isn't a streetlight to be seen. Instead the stars look down on us and lamp light flows out of the large living room window like a soft blanket over the arm of a chair. This is the kind of home that welcomes you in as you walk up the drive. Before you even open the front door you feel the same warmth that radiates from its owner moving delicately through the windchimes and evergreen leaves that line the path.

In her living room we sit with a teapot between us on the small coffee table, peppermint tea so we can still sleep tonight. I relax into the deep sofa and wrap a blanket round my legs. I am able to process the last twenty-four hours in the safety of this space. The words fall from my mouth, slowly at first and then a blizzard, drifting over the teapot and filling the room before escaping through the window into the night. There is no judgement from Annie, she just listens and nods her head in understanding and companionship. Teacup in hand, she passes her wisdom over to me wrapped in a peppermint mist. The events of yesterday feel far away, they are the past and all we have now is the future. Dwelling on who made what mistake and how things might have ended serves no one but the perpetually miserable.

The conversation flows away from distress as we settle into the rhythm of two friends talking. We are not concerned about the time or the now empty teapot. By the time we finish talking it is almost midnight. I leave my temporary shelter and walk to my car through the cold, clear air.

The frost on the grass is a mirror of the stars that now hold my secrets. The winter night no longer feels uncaring. It knows my pain and it welcomes me. The soft light of the living room lamp bathes my car in a warm embrace. Annie at the window watches me drive into the sympathetic darkness and waves goodbye in my rear-view mirror.

Author note: *This story was inspired by a period of time when I felt very lost. I was struggling with a terminally ill parent and I couldn't find the words to ask someone for help in guiding me through it. A friend from work was there for me when it got worse, and I still hold that evening close to my heart. I was sitting in a Tesco car park, and I just could not make myself go inside. After I called her she came and got me, we tackled the shopping together and then we had a pot of tea, and suddenly everything felt so much lighter.*

Thank You for Being a Friend
Stuart Knight

'These are memories that I'll wrap myself in when the world gets cold and I forget that there are people who are warm and loving.' – Dorothy Zbornak

Picture it. Fife. 2019. A baby English teacher hurtling towards early middle age takes his first steps into the world of rented accommodation. Crippled by loneliness and crushed by the weight of professional expectation, he finds comfort in the unlikeliest of companions: four fictional widows from a thirty-year-old, Miami-based sitcom. What can four old women from 1980s Florida teach a twenty-five-year-old man from Fife, you ask? Let me start at the beginning.

It was a year of firsts for me. My first year out of full-time education. My first year as a teacher. And eventually, my first flat. I had set sail from the safe harbour of my family home and voyaged towards the shiny new world of independent living.

The flat was my second-storey retreat from the world. A blank canvas that I could really put my stamp on. Two bedrooms, a modern kitchen, even a Juliet balcony where I could live out the fantasy of every Shakespeare-loving English teacher and regale the neighbourhood with my favourite soliloquies from Bill's back catalogue. No? Just me?

Most importantly, it was mine. Somewhere I could go to be alone, swaddled in the amniotic comfort of its beige walls. That was the plan, anyway. What I hadn't considered, in my semi-youthful naïveté, was the loneliness. I had been so keen to carve out an individual path and create a space that was all my own that I had forgotten that it would actually entail... well... being alone.

Meanwhile, work was no picnic. The first year of teaching is difficult and unforgiving. I'd work stressful eleven-hour shifts trying to meet expectations and fit in with colleagues and listen to an endless onslaught of 'he said' and 'she said' and the shrill bell screaming out relentlessly, and then return home to –

Silence.

Uncomfortable. Oppressive. Absolute. In time, my modern kitchen started to look a bit tired, my Juliet balcony started to look a bit vertiginous, and my blank canvas started to look a bit empty. A camping chair and a tiny TV were hardly the sophisticated single living I'd dreamed of. I'd find myself coming home to an empty house, working until the early hours and too busy to see friends. Racked with doubt, I started to question all of my choices.

Enter, *The Golden Girls*.

I'd heard of it, obviously, but I'd immaturely written it off as a show about old ladies. More fool me. This show was about to become my lifeline in choppy waters.

After a particularly awful day, I returned to my sparsely decorated abode. I'd made a sad little dinner, sat down on my sad little camping chair and watched something on my sad little telly. As the show faded to black, the first episode of *The Golden Girls* began to play and, too lazy to peel myself off the verdant canvas to fetch the remote, I watched it. In moments, I was immersed in the outrageous lives of Dorothy, Blanche, Rose and Sophia, and my grey world was transformed into glorious technicolour.

On paper, this was a mismatch. I wasn't a menopausal

widow navigating the trials and tribulations of learning to date again in my fifties. Our experiences were wildly different. But amid a personal storm, I'd washed up on a sunny Florida beach and found that their Miami home felt like the most stable place in the world. These fictional women were the reliable presence I desperately needed, and every time the theme song began to play, it was like slipping into a welcoming hug.

Before long, I was obsessed, and my late nights were accompanied by tall tales from Blanche's questionable Southern upbringing; my nagging doubts were assuaged by Rose's sunny outlook and stories from 'back in St Olaf'; my stress was eased by every comically pursed lip and raised eyebrow that Dorothy's face produced; and my fears were calmed by watching the zany schemes that Sophia enacted from beneath her (dreadful) wig.

'But it's a sitcom!' I hear you roar with pitying laughter. 'How can a sitcom compare to a real human connection?'

It can't. Obviously. But what's a friend if not someone who cheers you up and is there whenever you need them? Someone you learn from, grow with and are comforted by? At the most challenging time of my life, I wrapped myself in the Chanel-scented embrace of these women, and my outlook was all the better for it. So, what can four widows from 1980s Florida teach a crisis-ridden Fifer? Rather a lot, as it turns out.

The life I live today is worlds apart from the life I lived back then. I've settled into my career, moved house, made wonderful new friends and forged a meaningful relationship. Yet even with all of these positive developments, life is life. You make mistakes and fall flat on your face with frustrating regularity. But the balm that soothes the scars, and the resilience required to climb unsteadily back to my feet, is still in the gift of those four wonderful women, whose love and humour provided comfort at a time when such blessings were in relatively short supply.

Nowadays, the show is no longer a ritual. The sassy jokes no longer provide the background noise to my domestic life, and the theme music no longer punctuates my days. But every so often, on occasion, I switch on the TV and allow myself the luxury of a trip to Miami to be with friends. We venture out on the lanai, share a few stories, have a bite of cheesecake and soak up the Florida sunshine. The visits may be short, but as I bask in the warmth of these special and sacred moments, the world seems a little less cold, a little less lonely, and just a little more golden.

Author note: *After experiencing unexpected loneliness following a move into my own flat for the first time in 2019, I found comfort and unexpected friendship (of a sort) in the form of a cult 1980s sitcom.*

Don't Fear New Friends

Joanna Paul
Open Book Creative Writing Group

New person, their unfamiliar life situation.
There's a mechanism, a defence,
Ruling my space, flailing my confidence.
Heartbreaks can be platonic too.

Hesitate, bargain, deny:
Too old to try,
Life is on my mind,
Who has the time.

The walls grow tall,
Vulnerable happily hiding in their shadow.
Comfortable with ones it knows,
Terrified of ones outside the window.

Build new bridges, you know how.
Find a path through the rough.
Rusty latch on a dusty heart,
Lifted, it still works.

Soften your edges, notice,
Hovering over your threshold a warm heart,
Complete unknown with familiar eyes.
Let go, let them in, let it begin.

Share your love of books. . .

Scottish Book Trust is an independent national charity.
Our mission is to ensure people living in Scotland have
equal access to books.

If you've enjoyed this book, please consider making
a donation so that everyone in Scotland has the
opportunity to improve their life chances through books
and the fundamental skills of reading and writing.

Visit **scottishbooktrust.com/donate** to find out
more.

Previous editions

We have published an annual collection of stories like this one every year since 2009.

Days Like This (2009)
The Book That Changed My Life (2010)
Scottish Family Legends (2011)
My Favourite Place (2012)
Treasures (2013)
Scotland's Stories of Home (2014)
Journeys (2015)
Secrets and Confessions (2016)
Nourish (2017)
Rebel (2018)
Blether (2019)
Future (2020)
Celebration (2021)
Scotland's Stories (2022)
Adventure (2023)
Hope (2024)

Shop with Scottish Book Trust

Did you know we stock a wide range of book-related gifts for all ages on our online shop?

You'll find:
- Pin badges
- Tote bags
- Adult and children's book subscriptions
- Book nook kits
- Book lights
- Jigsaw puzzles
- Bookbug merchandise, including soft toys, stickers and stationery
- Books, soft toys, puzzles and games featuring classic children's book characters, including *The Gruffalo*, *Peter Rabbit*, *The Tiger Who Came to Tea* and *The Very Hungry Caterpillar*

All profits go back into our charity to help us continue to change lives with books.

Scan the QR code or visit **shop.scottishbooktrust.com** to browse our complete collection.